Rich Coach

Broke Coach™

150+ MISTAKES COACHES MAKE

Stop Wasting Time, Losing Money
& Maximize Your True Potential
As A Personal / Business Coach

BART SMITH

COPYRIGHT NOTICE

For more information about *150+ Mistakes Coaches Make*; individual orders; discounts for bulk-quantity purchases; audio training products; information on seminars; JV opportunities, mentoring/consulting; booking Bart Smith to speak at your next seminar, workshop or event; please contact the author at his website:

BARTSMITH.COM

VISIT BART ONLINE AT THESE SOCIAL PLATFORMS

 BartSmith.com/**youtube**

 BartSmith.com/**instagram**

 BartSmith.com/**tiktok**

 BartSmith.com/**linkedin**

TABLE OF "MISTAKES"

MISTAKES "BROKE" COACHES MAKE

W hat do they say about mistakes? They happen, right? Well, for coaches, we can't let too many mistakes happen or else we'll be out of business before we could say, "Whoops, I won't do that again."

Why be concerned about making mistakes?

Isn't failure feedback? Sure it is, but for coaches, minimizing the amount of times we fail or make mistakes will help keep us on track with our own goals as coaches, keep clients and prospects flowing in, keep clients moving towards their own goals with our help, and above all, keep our coaching businesses operating at optimal capacity. Now, if you don't watch out for them, well, you know what can happen:

CONSEQUENCES = OUCH!

So, the following common mistakes happen to all coaches at one time or another. As coaches, we must constantly be on the lookout for some of these mistakes and do our best to try to avoid them.

Whether you are a seasoned coach or new to coaching, my hope is that you will learn something new (or be reminded about something to watch out for) from this book to help you be even more successful in your coaching business pursuits!

But, here's the thing, the coaching profession continues to grow and evolve. New tools, new platforms, new technologies, and new ways of reaching and helping people are constantly appearing. While these innovations create exciting opportunities for coaches, they also introduce new ways to make mistakes.

In the pages ahead, you'll discover hundreds of common mistakes coaches make across every aspect of their profession — from running the business side of coaching, to working with clients, marketing your services, building your reputation, using modern technology, and much more.

You certainly don't have to make all of these mistakes yourself in order to learn from them. Instead, think of this book as a field guide to help you recognize potential pitfalls before they slow you down, cost you money, frustrate your clients, or derail your coaching career altogether. So, read through these pages carefully. Make note of the mistakes that stand out to you, and most importantly:

Do your best not to make them!

SO, ARE YOU READY? LET'S GET STARTED!

PART 1

Business Mistakes

BROKE COACHES MAKE

In no special order, here are a number of business mistakes coaches make that you might want to be aware of and hopefully avoid. Recognizing these common pitfalls early allows you to build a more resilient foundation and focus your energy on high-impact growth rather than preventable setbacks.

1. Failing to assess your coaching business when warning signs appear.

If you start to feel overworked, underpaid, overwhelmed, or out of control, it may be time to step back and evaluate how your business is structured. Many coaches push forward without pausing to examine what is working and what is not. When the workload grows but the income or satisfaction does not, that is a signal that something in the business model needs attention. Sometimes the answer is hiring help, improving systems, or narrowing your focus.

2. Constantly changing your business direction.

Some coaches rebuild their website, brand, services, or marketing strategy every few months. They jump from one tactic to another—social media today, webinars tomorrow, a new website design next month. This constant reinvention wastes time and money. Instead, simplify your approach and focus on consistent activities that bring clients into your world. Staying focused on a handful of proven actions usually produces better results than constantly chasing the next idea.

3. Not filling your calendar with activities that grow your business.

A successful coaching business rarely grows by accident. Your calendar should regularly include activities that expand your reach and reputation: writing books or articles, speaking, conducting webinars or workshops, networking with other professionals, and creating helpful content. When your schedule becomes empty or filled only with administrative tasks, growth slows down quickly.

4. Crossing professional boundaries with clients.

Maintaining professional boundaries protects both you and your client. Becoming emotionally or physically involved with clients can create ethical issues, misunderstandings, and even legal problems. You are dealing with people's hopes, fears, and sometimes very personal life situations. Maintaining a professional environment keeps the coaching relationship healthy and focused on the client's goals.

5. Not maintaining a financial reserve.

Every coaching business should maintain a financial cushion. Unexpected illness, vacation time, or temporary slow periods can interrupt your income. Setting aside several months of operating expenses provides peace of mind and stability. Without this reserve, a temporary slowdown can quickly turn into financial stress.

6. Waiting until you are busy to implement systems.

Many coaches wait until they are overwhelmed with clients before putting systems in place. The smarter approach is to build systems early—while you still have time. Scheduling tools, payment systems, contracts, email marketing platforms, and client management software can save enormous time later. When systems are in place before the rush begins, growth becomes much easier to manage.

7. Gossiping about clients.

Confidentiality is one of the foundations of coaching. Talking about clients—even casually with friends or colleagues—can destroy trust and damage your reputation. Clients share sensitive information with coaches. If they believe their personal situations might become conversation material for others, the coaching relationship quickly breaks down.

8. Ignoring legal protection.

Contracts, terms and conditions, and coaching agreements protect both you and your clients. Many new coaches overlook this area or assume nothing will go wrong. But misunderstandings, refund disputes, or unrealistic expectations can occur. Having clear legal agreements in place reduces risk and clarifies responsibilities.

9. Not clearly defining expectations with clients.

Clients should clearly understand what coaching includes and what it does not include. Coaching is not therapy. It is not consulting in every situation. It is a structured process designed to help clients move toward their goals. Clarifying roles and expectations prevents confusion later in the relationship.

10. Trying to build a coaching business alone.

Coaching can be a lonely profession when you attempt to build everything yourself. Connecting with other coaches creates opportunities for support, referrals, and collaboration. A network of professional peers can help you solve problems faster and avoid unnecessary mistakes.

11. Refusing to hire help when needed.

As your business grows, certain tasks should be delegated. Administrative work, website maintenance, graphic design, bookkeeping, and scheduling can consume valuable time. Hiring assistants or specialists allows you to focus on high-value activities like coaching and business development.

12. Ignoring the business side of coaching.

Many coaches enter the profession because they enjoy helping people. However, running a coaching practice is also running a business. Marketing, finances, taxes, and operations must be managed carefully. Coaches who ignore these areas often struggle to maintain steady income.

13. Operating without a business plan.

A business plan does not need to be complicated, but it should exist. Planning clarifies your target market, services, pricing, marketing strategies, and growth goals. Without a roadmap, many coaches wander from idea to idea without clear direction.

14. Poor organization and lack of task planning.

When there are no task lists, no planning system, and no structured workflow, coaches often become scattered. Important activities fall through the cracks. Organized systems—whether digital or paper—help maintain focus and productivity.

15. Keeping difficult clients too long.

Some clients create far more trouble than the value they bring. In certain situations, refunding the client and ending the relationship may protect your business and your reputation. Difficult clients can create unnecessary stress and even damage your credibility if conflicts escalate.

16. Allowing office clutter and disorganization.

A cluttered workspace can slow productivity and create unnecessary stress. Many coaches now operate nearly paperless offices using scanners, digital storage, and cloud systems. Reducing physical clutter allows you to focus more clearly on your work.

17. Not tracking income and expenses.

Every business owner must understand where money is coming from and where it is going. Regularly tracking financial activity helps you identify profitable services, control spending, and prepare for tax obligations.

18. Not tracking how your time is spent.

Time tracking reveals where productivity is lost. Many coaches are surprised when they discover how much time disappears into low-value activities instead of marketing, selling, and serving clients.

19. Seeing clients in your home.

Inviting clients into your home can blur professional boundaries and create unnecessary risks. Meeting clients in professional spaces—offices, coworking locations, or online sessions—usually maintains clearer structure.

20. Spending too little time on marketing.

Marketing is the engine of a coaching business. Without consistent outreach, visibility drops and new client opportunities disappear. Successful coaches dedicate significant time to attracting new prospects.

21. Not joining local business groups.

Local business communities often provide referrals, exposure, and valuable relationships. Many coaches overlook these opportunities and attempt to grow their business entirely online, missing potential connections nearby.

22. Not staying connected to industry associations.

Professional associations often provide continuing education, research, and networking opportunities. Staying connected to industry developments helps coaches remain informed and competitive.

23. Failing to protect your intellectual property.

If you create unique program names, frameworks, or branded coaching packages, consider protecting them legally when appropriate. Intellectual property can become a valuable asset as your reputation grows.

24. Giving assistants or designers too much control.

Always maintain ownership and access to your core systems— domain registrations, hosting accounts, payment systems, and client databases. Assistants and contractors should help manage these systems, but ultimate control should remain with you.

25. Offering services nobody is asking for.

Many coaches design services based on what they personally want to teach rather than what clients actually need. Market research and listening to client problems help shape services that people are willing to pay for.

26. Avoiding technology upgrades.

Modern tools often improve productivity and service quality. Updating software, platforms, and equipment periodically helps maintain efficiency and reliability.

27. Using your personal phone number for business.

Separating personal and business communication helps maintain boundaries. Many coaches use dedicated business phone numbers or call-forwarding systems.

28. Weak or unclear coaching agreements.

Coaching agreements should clearly define responsibilities, limitations, payment terms, and expectations. Well-written agreements prevent misunderstandings and protect both parties.

29. Not tracking coaching hours and client results.

Documenting the number of hours you have coached and the number of clients you have served can strengthen your credibility. These statistics demonstrate experience and commitment.

30. Trying to do everything yourself.

Delegating repetitive tasks allows you to focus on high-value work. Outsourcing certain activities can dramatically increase productivity and business growth.

31. Procrastinating on important business decisions.

Avoiding business tasks because they feel uncomfortable or unfamiliar can stall progress. Marketing, planning, and financial decisions require consistent attention.

32. Ignoring new ideas and innovations.

The coaching profession continues to evolve. New tools, platforms, and strategies regularly appear. Remaining curious and open to innovation helps coaches stay relevant and effective.

33. Not building automated scheduling systems.

Online scheduling tools simplify booking and reduce back-and-forth emails. Clients appreciate the convenience and professionalism.

34. Not creating a structured client onboarding process.

First impressions matter. A clear onboarding process—welcome materials, intake forms, expectations, and scheduling instructions—helps new clients start their coaching journey confidently.

35. Not documenting repeatable coaching frameworks.

Successful coaches often develop repeatable processes that guide clients through transformations. Documenting these frameworks makes your services easier to scale and teach.

36. Selling only one-on-one coaching.

Group programs, workshops, and digital resources allow coaches to help more people without increasing hours proportionally.

PART 2

Coaching/Client Mistakes

BROKE COACHES MAKE

1. Be mindful that even though you and your client might get along very well, and you might enjoy each other's conversations very much during the coaching process, it's results you're after.

Don't be hard on yourself or allow the client to get upset if things aren't progressing in the direction the client (or you) would like. The coaching process is quite different than how two people get along on a social level. Growth is a personal issue and must be appreciated for that difference.

2. Coaching is a sharing and watching activity.

As you share your knowledge and watch how a client responds, you might not be aware of what's really going on inside of the client that's preventing him/her from moving forward. It's then an issue of asking more questions, listening, and getting your client to be honest about what's really going on.

3. Not starting each session off with homework (if required), following up on that homework, making notes of each session, and requiring the client to do the same.

Without reviewing homework or session notes, you waste the first 15 minutes of every call just "catching up." By starting with the homework, you immediately ground the session in results and accountability rather than social pleasantries. Whats more, if you aren't making notes and requiring the client to do the same, your breakthroughs remain "oral traditions" that are easily forgotten. Writing it down forces the client to internalize the lesson and gives you a record to point back to when they feel stuck.

4. Giving clients short-term, quick-fix solutions for what really requires a long-term strategy to achieve long-term results.

While a quick fix makes the client feel better today, when the problem inevitably returns, they will blame your coaching. Short-term patches treat the symptoms, but long-term strategies solve the source. By pushing for the longer road, you position yourself as a high-level strategist rather than a mere "motivator," allowing you to charge for the massive life-shift you are actually facilitating.

5. Giving in to pressure, either generated by the coach from within or the client, to attain quick results.

Explain to clients that coaching is not a quick fix approach to improving any situation over the long haul. Coaching is about (slow and steady) growth and improving one's overall lifestyle/business with long-lasting outcomes.

6. Sharing your opinion about a topic too early in the coaching relationship.

Remember, coaching is 80% listening, and 20% asking questions and responding to what you've heard.

7. Being over anxious to solve, and not listening for more information.

From the coach's perspective, jumping to a solution too quickly is often a symptom of "expert's anxiety"—the pressure to prove your value by having all the answers immediately. When you rush to solve, you inadvertently shut down the client's process, potentially fixing the wrong problem because you didn't allow the full context to emerge. True authority comes from the confidence to sit in the silence and listen for the "problem beneath the problem," knowing that the most profound breakthroughs happen when you stop hunting for a quick win and start listening for the deeper patterns that only surface when a client feels truly heard.

8. Coaching in areas you're not trained in, authorized or licensed.

In this case, stop, tell the client "I don't think this is in the realm of my expertise, in fact, I might even have to be licensed to comment on that. Do you mind if I refer you to someone who is trained? I could make a personal introduction. I know a few people who could help you." Then, refund their money, because they'll need it where they're going. Hopefully, it's not too much of a refund. But, you get the idea. Don't swim in waters you're not trained in. You don't want to mess with the law, or advise them in a direction you're not qualified in just for the money. It's not worth it. Stay within what your coaching contract says you're able to coach on and no more.

9. Not pushing yourself (as a coach) to coach as much as you can, as often as you can, if you can, even for free.

Time in the saddle is what counts. This generates word-of-mouth testimonials for your good work, and confidence in you that you really can help people. Thinking about it when you're waiting for the phone to ring is one thing. Knowing it because you're in the zone with a client is another, whether it's a paid session or free one.

10. **Knowing the right answer, and giving it.**

Instead, keeping the right answer to yourself, and helping the client figure out the right answer on their own, no matter how long it takes. Coaching is a growing, learning process from within. Not a band aid approach from the outside. Coaches help their clients look within for the answers, not open you up like an encyclopedia for answers.

11. **Not adhering to a set of ethical standards as set by major coaching organizations, such as the International Coach Federation (ICF).**

If you don't know about it, you should. If you haven't read it, you should. If you don't follow it, you should. Visit their website   and   read   it: CoachFederation.org/ethics/. It's actually not that long. Read it, print it, memorize it.

12. **Not asking the client how you can best help them.**

Don't assume you know, ask!

13. **Not choosing to solve one problem at a time.**

Instead, some coaches try to take on too much with a client, never really finishing anything, only to leave the client frustrated and possibly asking for a refund for all that wasted time. Focus on one problem. Solve it. Then, introduce other services you have at that time. If a client asks, "What else do you do?" You can reply with what else you do, but gently insist you finish the first problem. "After we work on this first problem, we can move to the second. Let's stay organized and complete one thing first." (Client: "Makes sense. Okay."

14. Not clearly honing in on the client's problem up front, before a client enrolls in coaching with the coach.

This creates confusion and second thoughts whether the client should spend money up front. You should say, "I see what the problem is, I've dealt with this before, clients in the past have had great success with my coaching them through problem-x, why don't we get started today? Better to get your problem over with sooner, than later, right? Every day your problem is NOT solved, imagine the time and money you're losing. Put a value on your time (if money is not really a loss here). How much do you make? $75 an hour at your job? So, that's three months of struggling with this problem. That's 90 days (or more), and no weekends off. We never forget our problems. We take them home and to bed with us on our mind. So, 90 days x 24 hours a day x $75 per hour, I'd place a dollar value of that problem bothering you at around $162,000 worth of damage to your mind, spirit and such. I'm only charging you $1,500 for 10 sessions. That's a discount of over 90% off my regular coaching fee rates? You save over $160,000 .... I'm joking to make my point, and trying to put a dollar value on your problem/situation. What do you think about that. Is this a true value of the pain you're suffering with x-problem?"

15. Not firing a client, when they deserve to be.

Instead you keep them on for the money, but pay for it dearly in the long run. Offer 3-5 referrals so you show that you care about their growth, and want them to pick the best match for them. But, fire them.

16. Not giving the prospective client enough insight as to what a coaching session with you is like.

Record, in audio or video format, a 10-30 minute mock coaching session. If someone is in need of your services can sit down and watch you coach someone and really feel they're right there with you in the same room or on the phone, wow, that's powerful. They're ready to jump into your pool. All they need is a nudge in the form of a phone call, after they opted in to your list to view that video and you had a ASK ME ANYTHING BOX under the video where they dropped in their question and you called them back to say, "I got your question, would you like to talk about it?" That just opens the floodgates to clients opening up to you, and you working with them.

17. Not identifying and terminating (sooner than later) a client who is stubborn, argumentative, not willing to do the homework, shows signs of constant negativity.

These people, most likely, have other deeper rooted problems than you're prepared to handle or want to. So, do the right thing, and refund these people their money back, if any is refundable, and terminate this coaching relationship. This would be a good time to remind yourself to include a provision within your coaching client agreement that allows for you to make referrals to other coaches and even mental health counselors when needed.

18. Not recording your coaching telephone calls.

By NOT recording your calls, you have no record of what he said/she said. On the other hand, watch what YOU do say because it works both ways. You too are being recorded. Don't ever attempt to alter, tampered with, edit, erase or modify any audio recording of a conversation you might have with a coaching client. Do advise the client when you plan to record a session. It's the law!

19. **Not taking notes on your coaching sessions.**

Record your notes manually or on the computer. Make note of the date, topics discussed, advice YOU give, and anything important to the session. When you're on the phone with a client, typing can be distracting in the background, so in this case, while on the phone, it's best to hand write your notes in a journal, then transfer them to the computer when you end the call. You might share your notes with the client for his/her reaction and check-in to confirm or diffuse any discrepancies or misunderstandings.

20. **Not using forms, quizzes, charts, questionnaires or giving homework to help get to know the client.**

It's hard to play music or rehearse a speech just in your head. It's easier if you can read or see something written down before you following along towards the finish line of victory. While the "organic" approach builds rapport, using structured tools like forms and charts provides the data-driven foundation that allows a coach to scale their impact and accuracy with a client than just words coming out of their mouth or trying to read their mind as to who this client is and what are they all about.

21. **Taking on too many roles beyond their coach, like friend, therapist, dating, relationship/sexual interest, etc.**

Stay professional. Let them joke, but you stay professional. If they do joke about something you're uncomfortable with, ask them kindly not to think like that or talk about (something) in a manner that makes you feel uncomfortable. If you don't put the kibosh on it, they might keep pushing you in a direction that later you'll regret you didn't stop sooner when you had the chance.

22. Thinking it's your fault if clients don't succeed.

Clients own their success and failures 99%. You're just the driver's ed instructor sitting in the passenger seat. The client is still the driver.

23. Not defining communication rules.

With so many ways for people to communicate today, you don't want them knocking on all your doors and windows trying to talk to you. You're a paid coach for hire. So, state in your contracts how clients can contact you through methods such as eMail or telephone. There should be NO TEXTING unless it's an emergency for either parties and the only way to communicate when running late for there's a bonafide emergency. For example, "I can't call you right now, so I'm texting to say I must reschedule our time due to a family emergency. " OTHERWISE, you could get drawn into 20-30 texts per day from several clients. No texting. No instant messaging. Skype (and others) should be turned off. Log out of social media accounts when not in use. A client should have only contact information that you have set up. You might have all incoming calls go directly to voicemail so you can be prepared when responding to what questions or concerns when a client makes a request of your time. Remember, you set the rules for communication and time is money!

24. Over promising results.

It is better to under promise and over deliver. Deliver what you know you can coach actually offer and provide.

25. Not measuring client progress.

Many coaches talk about goals but never actually track whether progress is being made. Use simple metrics, milestone check-ins, or written progress summaries so clients can clearly see improvement over time.

26. Allowing unlimited access to you.

Some coaches promise clients they can text, email, or message anytime. Without clear boundaries this quickly leads to burnout and constant interruptions. Define specific communication channels and response times.

27. Letting coaching sessions drift without structure.

A coaching session should have direction. Without a loose agenda or focus, sessions can become casual conversations instead of meaningful progress toward the client's goals.

28. Failing to hold clients accountable.

Clients often know what they should do but struggle to follow through. A major part of coaching is helping clients stay accountable to the actions they commit to.

29. Not documenting your coaching frameworks.

Successful coaches usually develop repeatable methods or step-by-step frameworks. If your process only exists in your head, it becomes harder to scale your coaching or teach it to others. Documenting your unique "secret sauce" into a tangible system allows you to deliver consistent results for every client while freeing up your mental energy for deeper intuition. Furthermore, a formalized framework becomes a valuable intellectual property asset that can be packaged into books, courses, or group programs to grow your business beyond one-on-one sessions.

30. Talking more than the client.

Coaching is primarily about listening and asking thoughtful questions. When coaches dominate the conversation, clients lose the opportunity to discover their own insights.

31. Not setting clear objectives for each session.

Every session should begin with a clear objective or desired outcome. Without this focus, sessions may wander and valuable time may be lost.

32. Using AI tools improperly with clients.

AI tools can help generate ideas or reflection prompts, but they should never replace genuine coaching dialogue. Technology should support the coaching process, not substitute for human insight.

33. Not preparing before coaching sessions.

Reviewing previous notes, client goals, and recent progress before a session helps you guide the conversation effectively. Showing up unprepared can make coaching feel unstructured and unprofessional.

34. Allowing emotional dependency.

The goal of coaching is to help clients become stronger and more independent decision makers. If clients become overly dependent on the coach for every decision, growth slows and the relationship becomes unhealthy.

PART 3
Communication Mistakes
BROKE COACHES MAKE

Communication sits at the heart of every coaching relationship. Even the most skilled coaches can struggle to help clients if their communication style is unclear, inconsistent, or ineffective. The way you listen, ask questions, provide feedback, and guide conversations can dramatically influence your client's progress. The following mistakes highlight common communication pitfalls that can weaken trust, reduce clarity, and limit the impact of your coaching.

1. **Being Too Available!**

Ever just call up your favorite rock star and say, "Hey, when do you guys play next? Can I come to the show for free and visit you guys backstage where all the fun's at?" NO WAY! You can't even talk to them when you're in the same city as them. Why? Because they've created limited access to them. Why is this important for a coach? It's the HOOK syndrome we want to create. The NEED syndrome. You have to hook them into needing you so they don't come to think of you as a friend (who they DO call all the time for FREE). You charge for your time. You are a professional. Clients cannot just call you up and expect to talk to you like you're family/friends. That would also start them down the slippery slope of laziness. "My coach is my friend who doesn't care if I succeed or fail. I just enjoy talking to them whenever I want. They take my call and answer all my eMails within 24 hours. It's like having a new best friend." UH, NO! STOP THAT! DO NOT ANSWER THAT PHONE OR ANSWER THAT EMAIL WITHOUT PAYMENT. ;-) Now, use some latitude here and be the judge in your own situation, but you get the idea. Protect your time and then some!

2. Don't answer the phone when it rings.

Here's why ... Not answering the phones gives you time to think about what the caller is leaving in his/her voice message. You create that needed distance between you and the client. Think of your coaching business like a castle with a moat around you to protect your time and your wisdom. Not answering the phone allows you to stay organized. When clients call in, they know they have only 2-3 minutes to leave a message, so they get right to the point. By waiting to hear that message, you too can stay organized. Imagine answering all your calls and getting involved in long-winded conversations. No way, not you.

3. Finishing a clients' sentence is another mistake coaches make when communicating with their clients.

Let them finish 100% ... 100% of the time. This is for their sake, and yours, but mostly theirs. They must be responsible for completing what they think is the right response wholeheartedly. It's your job then to analyze what they said wholeheartedly and give them the proper feedback. If you finish their sentences for them, you are then only commenting on your words, not theirs. You get the idea.

4. Not able to express what they do and who their target market/client is in a clear, concise manner.

Instead, the coach is vague, boring, and non-specific in how they express what they do. "Hi, I'm a life coach." Uh, what? You're alive?

5. Talking too much during complimentary (free session) calls, and not asking enough questions and doing 80% of the listening (20% talking).

This is the best time to get clients into you by letting them pour out their heart and soul. When you listen more than you speak, you stop being a "salesperson" and start being a trusted mirror. By allowing a client to pour out their heart, you create a rare, safe space where they feel truly seen and understood for the first time. This 80/20 balance is the ultimate credibility signal. It proves you value their specific journey more than your own script. When they finally stop talking, they aren't just exhausted; they are emotionally invested in you because you held the space they desperately needed.

6. Telling clients everything that you do or know in a short span of time.

This is the fire hose method and it doesn't work. All it does is drown potential clients from talking to you, because they're too busy trying to survive the Niagara Falls worth of words you just poured on them. Instead, in your conversation, talk to people like watering small plants with a small amount of water. In order for the plant to truly absorb the water correctly, they have to get it in small amounts. Same with how we tell what we do or how we should coach a client. A little bit at a time. Best to ask questions and release bite-sized nuggets of what we do wrapped around a topic of conversation. Let it soak in and absorb. Only then are we much more effective as coaches.

7. Interrupting clients while they are speaking.

Allow clients to fully express their thoughts before responding. Interrupting breaks their train of thought and can prevent deeper insights from surfacing.

8. Using coaching jargon instead of clear language.

Clients may not understand specialized coaching terminology. Speak plainly and make sure your guidance is easy to understand and apply.

9. Sending overly long emails to clients.

Communication should be clear and concise. Long emails often overwhelm clients and reduce the likelihood that important points will be followed.

10. Failing to summarize what the client just said.

Repeating or summarizing a client's key points shows you are listening and helps confirm that you correctly understood their message.

11. Not setting expectations for response times.

Clients should know how quickly they can expect replies to messages or emails. Clear expectations prevent frustration and unnecessary follow-up messages.

PART 4

Education/Training Mistakes

BROKE COACHES MAKE

Continuous learning is important for every coach, but the way coaches pursue education and training can sometimes work against them. Many coaches spend too much time collecting certifications or studying new methods without fully applying what they already know. Others fail to stay current with new ideas, tools, and approaches that could improve their work. The following mistakes explore how coaches sometimes approach training in ways that slow their professional growth instead of strengthening it.

1. Failing to consume enough books, audio, and workshops to better yourself and your niche expertise limits the valuable stories and lessons you can share with your clients.

The tip here, never stop learning. You should be reading a minimum of one new book or eBook every 15-30 days, if not a couple at a time. Attend a minimum of 1-3 conferences per year.

2. Coaches don't have their own coach, mentor or adviser to help them grow in areas where they need help and growing.

Coaches don't have their own coach, mentor or adviser to help them grow in areas where they need help and growing. This creates a dangerous "blind spot" where a coach becomes trapped by their own limited perspective and unexamined habits. Without a mentor to provide an objective mirror, you risk stagnating in your development and failing to model the very commitment to growth that you demand from your own clients.

3. **Not getting certified.**

There are so many ways to get certified as a coach. If you don't qualify to get certified by some training programs, then choose to get certified in ways that you can quickly get certified. For example, some certification programs insist you have a certain number of hours already coached in order to get certified. You might not have enough hours to meet that certification. So, find another one that at least gives you certifiable training in another coaching discipline, skill or technique. When piled up, all those certifications make you a better coach, no doubt.

4. **Not hiring their own coach.**

If you are a coach and have never been coached yourself, get a referral to find a mentor coach. Find a coach who has been successfully working as a coach for several years. Ask if they'll coach you and offer you an inside look at what it's like to coach clients like those you want to coach.

5. **Not learning new tech skills.**

It has been five, even ten years, and you still don't know how to maintain your own website, set up a basic POP, alias email accounts, domain names, and more? You don't need to be super tech savvy to know these basic skills where you can save $$$$$$!

6. **Not adding new "niche" coaching services to your present one to add to your income base.**

Without spreading yourself too thin, you might pick up a new specialty in a niche coaching area that complements the one you're already providing. To do this, head back to new workshops, training programs, courses, certifications, etc.

7. Stopping your learning after becoming a coach.

Coaching skills should evolve constantly. Reading, attending workshops, and studying new approaches keeps your thinking fresh and your coaching relevant. When you stop being a student, your sessions become predictable and your frameworks grow stagnant, eventually failing to meet the complex, shifting needs of your clients. True authority is maintained by staying at the cutting edge of your field, ensuring you always have a "walking encyclopedia" of new stories and strategies to offer those who trust you with their growth.

8. Ignoring new research in psychology and behavior change.

Modern coaching overlaps with fields like psychology, neuroscience, and habit formation. Staying informed about these areas strengthens your coaching insights. By understanding the biological and mental drivers behind human behavior, you can offer clients evidence-based strategies that lead to more sustainable, long-term change. This interdisciplinary approach moves you beyond generic motivation and positions you as a sophisticated expert capable of navigating the complex mechanics of the human mind.

9. Not investing in specialized training within your niche.

General coaching knowledge is helpful, but niche expertise often makes a coach far more valuable to specific types of clients. When you specialize, you stop competing on price and start competing on the unique depth of your specific results, allowing you to speak directly to a client's secret frustrations and precise goals. This targeted focus transforms you from a "luxury" into a "necessity" for those who need an expert who already speaks their language and has mastered their specific challenges.

10. Learning but never applying what you study.

Many coaches consume books, courses, and seminars but fail to apply the lessons, often falling into the trap of "passive learning" where they collect information rather than integrating it. Education only becomes valuable when it changes how you work with clients, shifting from mere intellectual theory into a practical tool that produces tangible results.

Without this critical bridge between consumption and implementation, a coach risks becoming a walking library of unused potential rather than an active agent of transformation. True mastery requires you to filter every new insight through the lens of your client's specific needs, ensuring that every page read or workshop attended directly enhances the wisdom, stories, and frameworks you bring to your next session.

11. Relying only on free information online.

Free content can be helpful, but serious professional growth often requires investing in structured training, mentors, and higher-level programs. Relying solely on fragmented, free information often leads to a "patchwork" education that lacks the cohesion and depth necessary for true mastery. By putting skin in the game through paid resources, you gain access to the proprietary systems and direct feedback that shortcut your learning curve and separate the hobbyists from the elite experts.

PART 5

Marketing Mistakes

BROKE COACHES MAKE

Many coaches believe that once they become skilled at coaching, clients will naturally find them. Unfortunately, building a successful coaching practice requires more than talent—it requires effective marketing. Coaches who ignore marketing or approach it inconsistently often struggle to attract the clients they want to serve. The following mistakes highlight common marketing missteps that can limit visibility, slow business growth, and prevent great coaches from reaching the people who need them most.

1. Letting the competition get to your self-confidence or ability to get out there.

There is no competition, you hear? None. There is only you, and if clients want someone like you, a unique individual with unique gifts and a unique way of looking at/solving problems, then there's no question, you will be hired. But, they (clients) need to know about you. Why aren't you out there? So, not getting out there is problem #1, and #2 is worrying about the competition. Did the Rolling Stones worry about the Beatles? Did Elvis Presley worry about Frank Sinatra? Did Carl's Jr. worry about McDonald's? Then, why are you worrying about so and so and you know who? Stop that. No more! Get out there. The world is waiting to meet someone exactly like you!

2. Not attending enough events where you can network with others.

Not finding a quiet space in the corner of the room, lobby or hotel, where you can have people come meet with you for 5-10 minutes each. These are quick power coaching sessions, where they tell you the one thing that's on their mind (i.e., pain/problem/passion), of which you also got them fired up with a handout you gave them earlier to prepare for this 5-10 minute power coaching session. In doing this they get excited, get to try you out, you get to meet them, look them in the eye, etc. Let them talk 80% of the time, while you chime in for the remaining 20%. It's easy to RUN OUT OF TIME, and say, "Would you like to continue this during a real 1-hour free session? Talk about an already warm lead. Do this to 5-25 people at such an event and see how many warm leads you actually get. It might take you an hour or two to get those 5-25 leads, but it's worth it. You know about rapid dating or speed dating? This is called "speed coaching!" Same concept!

3. Boring website, boring copy, boring photos, boring anything and everything, are more mistakes coaches make.

Also, being cliché, using predictable phrases, general statements, etc. Not you. NEVER be this way.

4. Not donating time for charity work.

Here's why this is important. Are you only in it for the money or do you really want to help people? Chances are, if you're not paid, you won't coach. Sure, you have a burning desire to help others. Okay, put your money where you mouth is and do some charity work. For starters, this gets you away from the work-zone into a true helping others zone. Next, that photo of you dishing out those turkey legs at that homeless shelter really resonates with that corporate client who was looking for someone to hire for their personal coaching needs. Seeing you helping others is just the kind of big heart most clients need to know when they hire you. Are you all about the money? Or is there another side of you that really does care about people? You only have to donate an afternoon once or twice a year for this to have its affect. It could be for seniors, homeless, veterans, animals, children, half-way houses, domestic violence shelters, etc. Find ten different causes in your area, and participate in one of them every other month or so. Up to you, but I think you get where this can lead to. Besides, what a great way for you to get endorsements from those organizations for your website. "Susan Smith, Professional Coach at www.HerSite.com, donated her time to help _____ [name of organization]." If your name goes on their website, look out for some great search engine back links to your website hopefully. The potential is unlimited.

5. **Not learning everything you can about (and using) social media (i.e., Facebook, LinkedIn, Instagram, Pinterest, Twitter, etc.) to promote your coaching business.**

Failing to master social media means losing the primary platform where modern clients verify your legitimacy before ever booking a call. Without a strategic social presence, you risk becoming "invisible" to a global audience that increasingly uses these platforms as a search engine for expertise.

6. **Looking at marketing as work.**

It's not. Marketing can be (and is) FUN! Marketing is an activity and an excuse to PARTY! Why? Marketing gets you away from what's boring to what's exciting, which is interacting with people and promoting your business.

7. Make it easy for clients to give you testimonials.

For starters, most people are not good at writing, let alone how they feel about what you did for them as your coach. So? Help them. Ask them these three very basic questions, and then YOU formulate their testimonial out of their own words.

8. NOT writing a book.

For a personal coach, not writing a book is more than just a missed creative opportunity; it is a strategic disadvantage that limits your growth, income, and credibility in a crowded market. In the coaching world, a book is often seen as the "new minimum expectation" for those taking their business to the next level. Without one, you may be perceived as "just another coach" rather than a leading authority.

9. Not making videos about your coaching passion to reach potential clients.

In the modern market, video is the closest thing to a face-to-face meeting. By refusing to get in front of a camera, you are essentially leaving a "personality gap" that written words alone can't fill. Shy? Let AI be your clone and speak for you so you don't have to. Check out HeyGen.com and all its possibilities.

10. Not FILLING UP their calendar with marketing activities to bring in new business.

Failing to "fill your calendar" with marketing activities means you are essentially operating a hobby, not a business. If you aren't actively generating demand, you are relying entirely on hope and luck, which is a recipe for professional burnout and financial instability.

11. **NOT telling people what you do NOT do.**

You're quick to explain exactly what you do, but you neglect to define your boundaries and specify what you don't do, which is essential for protecting your valuable time.

12. **Not following-up with client prospects you met.**

Do not assume they'll call you or they're reading your material and need more time. Reach out to them after 1-2 weeks, 3-4 weeks, 1-2 months.

13. **Not disqualifying (wrong) candidates for coaching and turning them away before you get hooked into working with them only to let them go later, and possibly at a higher price.**

Working with someone who isn't a fit—whether due to a lack of commitment, a personality clash, or being outside your niche—is exhausting. This "friction" bleeds into your sessions with good clients, lowering the quality of your overall work.

14. **Not getting prospects to consume you first on their time with something free.**

They come to you, or you go to them, unprepared in the sense that they don't really know much about you or have experienced you. Increase your odds at closing the sale by offering them an inside peek to a sample coaching session. This can be a simple 15-30 minute audio recording outlining a specific problem and how you would go about handling it.

15. Not providing for, asking, inserting, or remembering to put a call-to-action at every turn of your world as a coach.

That means, at the end of every article, chapter, video, podcast, audio track ... CALLS-TO-ACTION EVERYWHERE! By consistently providing a clear "next step," you transform passive consumers into active leads who are ready to engage with your expertise.

16. Not starting your own podcast or being interviewed on other people's podcast to promote your coaching business.

Ignoring the power of podcasting is like being an expert who refuses to pick up a megaphone in a crowded room. In a relationship-based business like coaching, your voice is your greatest conversion tool. Hosting your own podcast establishes you as an authoritative voice in your niche, allowing you to showcase your expertise and build deep, authentic trust with your audience through the intimacy of audio. It serves as a powerful lead generation tool that warms up potential clients by providing consistent value, while simultaneously expanding your professional network through high-level guest interviews. Furthermore, podcasting creates a library of evergreen content that can be repurposed across social media, helping you scale your personal brand and reach a global audience without the constant need for one-on-one discovery calls.

17. Not using autoresponders to follow-up with potential clients via eMail to help schedule a complimentary session.

Failing to use autoresponders means you are relying on your own memory to handle the most critical part of your sales funnel—the follow-up. This manual approach is a "silent killer" of growth because most clients don't book on the first visit; they require multiple touchpoints before they feel safe enough to schedule a session.

18. Not utilizing mobile phone (and other portable devices) and mobile apps to help promote their coaching services and service their clients at the same time.

Using mobile phone apps, or developing your own, you could acquire more leads, increase client engagement, build brand awareness/loyalty, promote/sell your products, deliver your coaching messages to your clients on these portable devices building greater client-retention, and above all add more revenue to your current coaching business stream of income.

19. Not writing articles, and working with reporters to help boost your own credibility in the media (=exposure) which trickles down to generating leads then into sales..

20. Relying on you, personally and manually, to follow-up with, check in, and remind coaching clients about sessions, to sign-up, take action, etc.

Automate these tasks with the right online system/software or hire someone to make calls for you.

21. Starting with the one marketing activity you love most, and not the ones that will really generate the results you need.

Doing the uncomfortable (marketing tasks) will make your LIFE comfortable. Do the comfortable, and your life will be uncomfortable. Simple formula.

22. Not continuing to market and brand themselves to get their name out there.

Think of actors and actresses back a few years ago who we haven't seen since? Where are they? What are they up to? NO ONE KNOWS. NO ONE CARES. Out of sight, out of mind. You never know when you'll have a dip in client sign ups. It will be great to still have your marketing machine running out there for your benefit in securing new clients.

23. Thinking that you don't need a book to promote your coaching business.

A book transforms your coaching practice by serving as the ultimate credibility signal, instantly establishing you as a "walking encyclopedia" in your niche. It acts as a high-level marketing tool that pre-sells your methodology, allowing prospects to experience your unique insights before ever booking a session. By providing a scalable way to reach global audiences and opening doors to speaking engagements and media opportunities, a book turns your expertise into a tangible asset that attracts high-value clients and solidifies your authority in the marketplace.

24. Thinking that you're selling coaching services.

You're not selling coaching services, you are selling solutions. Try to put yourself in your client's shoes and look at their world from their perspective. Brainstorm with your client and talk in terms of results, dreams, desired outcome, ambitions, accomplished goals, etc.

25. Waiting until all your marketing materials are perfect to start marketing.

Waiting until your marketing materials are perfect is a trap because perfection is a moving target that only reveals itself through real-world feedback. In the coaching world, "perfect" materials created in a vacuum often miss the mark; you only learn what actually resonates with your audience by putting content out and seeing what sticks.

26. Worrying that you aren't that engaged or using social media, or you don't have enough likes, fans, posts or activities to build a personal bond with total strangers.

Should you even use social media to promote your business? Yes, but you must have a social media strategy to expand your business and engage in innovative and meaningful ways. Focus on the fundamentals of marketing and devote your time up front to nurturing other marketing tactics.

27. Ignoring email list building.

An email list remains one of the most reliable marketing assets. Coaches who rely only on social media platforms risk losing contact with their audience if algorithms change.

28. Not creating valuable content regularly.

Articles, videos, podcasts, and short insights help potential clients learn from you before they hire you. Consistent content builds authority and trust.

29. **Failing to clearly define a niche market.**

When a coach tries to help everyone, the message becomes weak. Clear niche positioning helps prospects immediately recognize that you understand their problems.

30. **Not tracking which marketing efforts actually produce clients.**

Many coaches spend time on marketing activities but never measure results. Tracking where leads come from helps you focus on the strategies that truly work. Without this data, you are essentially gambling with your time, repeating efforts that may yield zero return while neglecting the specific channels that actually convert. By implementing simple tracking systems, you can stop the "guesswork" and confidently double down on the high-impact actions that build your authority and grow your bank account.

31. **Relying only on social media for marketing.**

Social media is useful, but it should not be the only marketing channel. Books, speaking, articles, email lists, partnerships, and referrals should also be part of your strategy.

PART 6

Mindset
Mistakes

BROKE COACHES MAKE

A coach's mindset plays a powerful role in how they run their business, serve their clients, and respond to challenges. Doubt, fear, and limiting beliefs can quietly influence decisions and hold coaches back from reaching their full potential. At the same time, a strong and confident mindset can help coaches navigate obstacles and build lasting success. The following mistakes reveal how mindset issues can interfere with progress and what coaches should watch for as they grow their careers.

1. Buying every new book or training program thinking it's the golden ticket to making money and finding clients.

Many coaches fall into the trap of believing the next book, course, or certification will magically solve all their business problems. Continued learning is valuable, but no training program replaces consistent action. The old-fashioned fundamentals still matter: talking to people, asking for referrals, creating content, marketing your services, and building real relationships. If you spend all your time buying information and very little time applying it, you stay busy without becoming profitable.

2. Giving up too soon when moments of doubt creep in.

Every coach has moments of uncertainty. The problem is not doubt itself — it is quitting because of doubt. Building a coaching business takes persistence, repetition, and faith in your ability to improve. If you give up every time things feel hard, you never stay in the game long enough to develop real momentum. Keep going, keep learning, and remember that many successful people looked unsure before they looked established.

3. Looking at selling as something bad.

Sales is not about tricking people or pressuring them into something they do not want. Sales is about helping someone make a decision that may improve their life or business. If you genuinely believe your coaching can help someone, then learning how to explain your value and ask for the sale is part of serving them well. Coaches who see sales as something dirty often sabotage their own income and limit the number of people they can help.

4. Not asking for what you want, when you know what you need.

Many coaches stay quiet when they should be speaking up. They do not ask for referrals, introductions, interviews, speaking opportunities, or partnerships because they fear rejection. Yet the people who grow fastest are often the ones willing to ask. If you want new opportunities, you have to put your requests into the world. No one can say yes to what you never ask for.

5. Not valuing what you bring to the table.

Your knowledge, experience, frameworks, tools, and guidance all have value. Too many coaches downplay what they offer because helping others comes naturally to them. But just because something feels natural to you does not mean it is common or easy for others. The results you help create deserve to be exchanged for money. When you undervalue your expertise, clients may undervalue it too.

6. Not thinking like a business owner or CEO.

A hobby is something you squeeze in when you have time. A business is something you build with intention, structure, and responsibility. If you want coaching to become a real source of income, you must think like the person in charge of a company. That means making decisions, tracking numbers, planning ahead, marketing consistently, and treating your work as something serious. Coaches who think like hobbyists rarely create sustainable businesses.

7. Trying to be all things to all people.

When you try to help everybody, your message becomes weak and your marketing loses power. It is much easier to attract clients when people immediately understand who you help and what problems you solve. Narrowing your focus does not shrink your business — it makes your expertise easier to recognize. A clear niche often leads to more confidence, better referrals, and stronger results.

8. Letting doubt and overwhelm build up without taking care of yourself.

When coaches feel overwhelmed, they sometimes keep pushing without pausing to reset. That can lead to exhaustion, low confidence, and poor decision-making. One of the best ways to combat self-doubt is to remind yourself of the value you bring and the progress you have already made. Write down your strengths, the wins you have helped clients achieve, and the qualities people consistently appreciate in you. Read that list when your confidence drops.

9. "I don't know how to tell people what I do."

If you cannot clearly explain what you do, who you help, and why it matters, your business will struggle. This is not a permanent weakness — it is simply a communication skill that can be improved with practice. Rehearse your explanation until it becomes natural and clear. The more clearly you describe your coaching work, the easier it becomes for the right people to understand why they should hire you.

10. "I don't really know how to coach someone, but I like the idea of being a coach."

Liking the idea of being a coach is not the same as being prepared to coach effectively. If you feel uncertain about your actual coaching ability, that is a sign to train, practice, observe other coaches, and get experience. Confidence grows through action and repetition. The solution is not to hide from the work, but to learn the craft and improve with every client conversation.

11. "I hate sales, and I hate to push my coaching on anybody."

This belief often sounds noble, but it can become an excuse for avoiding necessary business activity. If someone has a real problem and you have a real solution, inviting them to work with you is not pushing — it is offering help. The key is to ask questions, listen carefully, and connect your coaching to the results they want. Clients expect professionals to discuss fees and next steps. Do not make it awkward by treating money as forbidden.

12. "I'm afraid of marketing and admittedly I procrastinate and prefer to hide out."

Marketing fear is one of the most common mindset challenges coaches face. Many want clients, but do not want to risk visibility, criticism, or rejection. The truth is, if you believe in the value of your coaching, then marketing is simply the process of letting people know you exist. You do not need to market perfectly — you just need to market consistently. Visibility creates opportunity.

13. Comparing your progress to other coaches.

Comparison can quietly destroy momentum. When you constantly measure your progress against other coaches, you may overlook how much you have already grown. There will always be someone further ahead, louder, richer, or more established. Focus on building your own business, serving your own audience, and improving your own systems. Comparison steals energy you could be using to move forward.

14. Waiting to feel confident before taking action.

Confidence usually comes after action, not before it. Many coaches wait until they feel fully ready to market, raise prices, launch offers, or speak publicly. That delay keeps them stuck. The more you act, the more evidence you build that you can handle what comes next. Confidence is often the reward for courage, not the prerequisite.

15. Thinking success must happen quickly.

A coaching business rarely becomes strong overnight. It usually grows through consistent effort, repeated learning, and patient refinement over time. Coaches who expect instant success often become discouraged and quit too early. The better mindset is to think long term. Build momentum month by month, not fantasy by fantasy.

16. Allowing criticism to stop your progress.

The moment you become visible, someone will disagree with you, question you, or criticize you. That is normal. Useful criticism can help you improve, but pointless negativity should not control your behavior. Coaches who let criticism shut them down often disappear before they ever gain traction. Learn from what is helpful and ignore what is not.

17. Believing you must be perfect before helping others.

Perfectionism delays action and kills progress. You do not have to know everything before you can help someone take the next step. Clients are not looking for a flawless human being. They are looking for someone who can guide them, encourage them, and help them make progress. Keep improving, but do not wait for perfection before serving people.

PART 7

Money-Making
Mistakes

BROKE COACHES MAKE

Many coaches enter the profession with a sincere desire to help others—but very little preparation for the financial realities of running a business. As a result, they often struggle not because they lack coaching skill, but because they make avoidable money-related mistakes. These mistakes can limit income, reduce stability, and prevent a coaching practice from reaching its full potential. The following mistakes highlight some of the most common ways coaches unintentionally hold themselves back financially—and what you should be aware of if you want to build a coaching business that is both meaningful and profitable.

1. Thinking clients will refer you business just because you did a good job with them.

Referrals rarely happen automatically. Even satisfied clients need reminders and encouragement to refer others to you. Successful coaches intentionally build referral systems by asking for introductions, requesting testimonials, and reminding clients that referrals are welcome. If you rely solely on goodwill without actively asking, you will miss many opportunities to grow your business.

2. Losing clients or turning them away because you don't have additional products or programs.

Many coaches lose revenue simply because they have nothing else to offer once a coaching program ends. Workshops, courses, books, membership programs, and digital resources allow clients to continue learning from you while generating additional income. Without these options, clients leave even though they may still want guidance.

3. Asking clients what they would pay for your services.

Allowing clients to determine your price usually results in undervaluing your work. Most people price things based on what they can afford rather than the true value of the service. As the professional, it is your responsibility to set your rates based on your expertise, results, and market demand. Let the market respond to your pricing rather than letting the client set it.

4. Coaching primarily because you need the money.

If money becomes your primary motivation, it can affect how you interact with clients. Coaching works best when the focus is on helping people achieve meaningful results. When you prioritize service first and money second, your reputation and client success grow—and the income usually follows naturally.

5. Giving away too many discounts or free sessions.

Occasional promotional sessions are fine, but too many free or discounted sessions weaken your business model. Set a clear limit for how many discounted sessions you will offer each year. When that limit is reached, you must return to your normal rates to maintain a sustainable business.

6. Bartering services too often instead of charging fees.

Trading services may seem appealing, but it often leads to complicated arrangements and reduced income. While occasional bartering may work in specific situations, your primary business model should involve clear pricing and payment. Boundaries help maintain professionalism and ensure your time is properly valued.

7. Not generating enough leads per month.

No coaching business survives without a steady stream of potential clients. Lead generation must be a consistent activity, not something you only think about when business slows down. Networking, content marketing, speaking, writing, and partnerships are just a few ways to continuously bring new prospects into your pipeline.

8. Not writing a book.

Writing a book is one of the fastest ways to establish credibility and visibility as a coach. A book demonstrates expertise, helps attract media attention, and can lead to speaking engagements, workshops, and consulting opportunities. It also allows your ideas to reach far more people than one-on-one coaching alone.

9. Not bundling your products with others.

Collaborating with complementary experts allows you to reach new audiences and create bundled offers that provide greater value to customers. Product bundles, joint programs, and partnership promotions can significantly increase exposure and revenue while sharing marketing efforts with others.

10. Not building your coaching business with the possibility of selling it someday.

Many coaches never consider that their business could become a valuable asset. Systems, strong branding, repeatable processes, and a loyal client base can make a coaching practice attractive to buyers. Thinking long-term encourages you to build a business that has lasting value.

11. Not creating products to supplement your coaching income.

You cannot coach clients every hour of every day. Books, courses, workshops, and digital products allow you to earn income even when you are not actively coaching. Product development also helps scale your knowledge to a larger audience.

12. Not learning the art of sales.

Marketing brings attention to your services, but sales convert that attention into income. Many coaches avoid sales conversations because they feel uncomfortable discussing money. Learning how to confidently explain your value and guide clients toward decisions is essential for building a profitable practice.

13. Not licensing your successful systems or materials.

If you develop tools, worksheets, or processes that work well for your clients, consider licensing them to other coaches. Licensing allows you to earn additional income while expanding your influence and reputation within your industry.

14. Not making list-building a top priority.

An email list is one of the most valuable assets in your business. It allows you to communicate directly with potential clients and stay connected with past customers. Coaches who consistently grow their lists have a much easier time promoting programs, products, and events.

15. Not providing paid follow-up resources like audio downloads.

Clients often want reinforcement after a coaching session. Audio recordings, summaries, or downloadable resources provide additional support while creating another revenue opportunity. These resources also help clients revisit key lessons between sessions.

16. Not recording coaching calls or workshops for future revenue.

Coaching sessions and workshops contain valuable insights that can be repurposed into training materials. Recording these sessions allows you to create courses, downloadable programs, or membership content that continues generating income long after the event ends.

17. Not learning to create your own marketing and training materials.

Being able to produce your own presentations, worksheets, and promotional materials reduces costs and speeds up your ability to launch programs. Basic design and content skills allow you to bring ideas to life quickly.

18. Not brainstorming new ideas regularly.

Innovation often leads to the most profitable opportunities. Successful coaches continually explore new ways to deliver their knowledge—whether through programs, partnerships, products, or services.

19. Not training other coaches to expand your model.

If your methods produce strong results, you may be able to train other coaches to deliver your system. Certification programs or licensed coaching models can significantly expand your reach and revenue.

20. Not using objections as opportunities to improve your sales conversations.

Client objections often reveal what prospects need to hear in order to feel confident moving forward. Instead of viewing objections as rejection, treat them as feedback that helps you refine your messaging and communication.

21. Not repurposing your content into multiple formats.

One idea can become many assets. A single concept can turn into a blog post, video, workshop, book chapter, or online course. Repurposing allows you to maximize the value of your expertise.

22. Pricing products too high instead of using them as entry points.

Low-priced products often serve as gateways to higher-value programs. A book or small course can introduce clients to your work and build trust before they invest in coaching services.

23. Spending too much time learning and not enough time earning.

Continued education is valuable, but it should not replace action. Many coaches stay in perpetual training mode instead of applying what they have learned. Balance education with real-world implementation.

24. Relying 100% on coaching income.

Depending entirely on hourly coaching limits your earning potential. Diversifying income through products, courses, and events creates more stability and scalability.

25. Not turning your coaching knowledge into workshops or programs.

Workshops and structured programs allow you to help many people at once while increasing revenue. They also establish you as an authority in your field.

26. Competing on price instead of value.

Lowering your prices to compete with others can damage your perceived value. Focus on the results you provide rather than trying to be the cheapest option available.

27. Not believing you can turn small customers into long-term clients.

A small purchase often begins a long-term relationship. Clients who first encounter your work through a book, webinar, or entry-level program may eventually become high-value coaching clients.

28. Feeling uncomfortable making money.

Money should be viewed as a natural result of delivering value. When coaches feel guilty about charging fees, they often sabotage their own success.

29. Undervaluing and undercharging for your services.

Many professionals underestimate the value of their knowledge and experience. Charging appropriately not only supports your business but also signals confidence and professionalism.

30. Not turning clients into long-term customers.

Client relationships should extend beyond a single program whenever appropriate. Follow-up services, advanced programs, and ongoing support help create lasting partnerships.

31. Believing you shouldn't charge because you care about clients.

Caring about people and charging for your expertise are not mutually exclusive. In fact, when clients invest financially, they often commit more fully to the process and achieve stronger results.

PART 8

Personal Mistakes

BROKE COACHES MAKE

Running a coaching business doesn't just require professional skills—it also requires personal discipline, organization, and self-awareness. The way you manage your time, energy, relationships, and daily habits can directly influence how successful and sustainable your coaching practice becomes. The following mistakes highlight personal behaviors that can quietly hold coaches back if left unchecked.

1. Mixing socially with your clients.

Maintaining professional boundaries is important in coaching relationships. Socializing in ways that blur professional lines can create confusion about the coach–client relationship and weaken your authority as a coach.

2. Neglecting your own well-being and self-care.

A coach who is exhausted, stressed, or burned out cannot effectively guide others. Taking care of your physical and mental health allows you to show up fully for your clients.

3. Not performing self-assessments on your coaching skills.

Coaches should regularly evaluate their own performance, methods, and results. Honest reflection helps identify areas for improvement and ensures that you continue growing as a professional.

4. Neglecting the needs of your friends and family.

Coaches often invest large amounts of emotional energy in their clients. It is important to remember that your family and close relationships also need your time, attention, and support.

5. Failing to set clear personal boundaries with clients.

Without boundaries, clients may expect access to you at all hours. Clear expectations about communication times, session limits, and availability protect both your personal life and your professional credibility.

6. Trying to solve every client problem personally.

Coaches sometimes feel responsible for fixing everything in a client's life. Your role is to guide, challenge, and support—not to carry every burden your client faces.

7. Taking client setbacks personally.

Clients may struggle, regress, or fail to follow through on goals. Coaches should support and guide them without internalizing these setbacks as personal failures.

8. Not continuing your own personal development.

A coach who stops growing eventually loses perspective and effectiveness. Reading, training, reflection, and new experiences help keep your coaching fresh and relevant.

9. Allowing coaching to consume your entire identity.

When your entire identity becomes wrapped up in coaching, it becomes difficult to maintain balance. Healthy interests, hobbies, and relationships outside of coaching keep your life grounded.

10. Avoiding honest feedback about your coaching.

Constructive criticism from peers, mentors, or clients can help improve your practice. Coaches who avoid feedback often stop evolving professionally.

PART 9

Social Media Mistakes

BROKE COACHES MAKE

Social media is a powerful tool for building authority and connecting with clients, yet many coaches struggle without a clear strategy. This lack of planning leads to wasted effort and missed opportunities. By avoiding common online mistakes, you can increase your visibility and effectively grow your coaching business.

1. Failing to create a social media strategy.

Many coaches post randomly without a clear plan for what they want to achieve. A strategy helps you decide what platforms to use, what type of content to create, and how often you will post. Planning your content weeks or even months in advance makes your social media activity more organized and effective.

2. Trying to master every social media platform at once.

Attempting to dominate every platform often spreads your time and energy too thin. It is usually better to focus on one or two platforms where your target audience spends time. Once you gain traction and develop a consistent system, you can expand to additional platforms.

3. Not using live streaming to connect with your audience.

Live video allows people to interact with you in real time and experience your personality and coaching style. This kind of interaction builds trust quickly and can turn casual viewers into potential clients.

4. Posting inconsistently on social media.

Inconsistent posting makes it difficult for audiences to stay connected with you. Regular activity helps you stay visible and reinforces your authority in your coaching niche.

5. Not collaborating with other coaches or influencers.

Partnerships expose you to new audiences and expand your reach. Joint livestreams, shared content, and collaborative promotions can dramatically increase visibility.

6. Not studying what successful coaches are doing online.

Observing successful coaches can provide valuable insights into what types of content attract attention and engagement. You do not need to copy others directly, but studying their strategies can inspire ideas for your own content.

7. Not using visual storytelling like infographics, images, and videos.

Visual content often performs better than plain text posts. Infographics, images, short videos, and visual demonstrations help communicate ideas quickly and capture attention.

8. Not creating videos that demonstrate your coaching style.

Video allows people to see how you communicate, teach, and guide others. Demonstrating your coaching approach builds credibility and helps potential clients decide whether you are the right coach for them.

9. Failing to review social media analytics.

Analytics show which posts perform well and which ones do not. By reviewing engagement, reach, and follower growth, you can refine your strategy and focus on the content that resonates with your audience.

10. Not focusing on a specific niche audience.

Trying to appeal to everyone often results in content that attracts no one in particular. When you focus on a specific niche, your message becomes clearer and more appealing to the people you want to serve.

11. Creating content that doesn't educate, entertain, or empower.

Effective social media content typically falls into three categories: educational, entertaining, or empowering. Posts that combine these elements tend to attract attention and keep audiences engaged.

12. Not setting goals for follower or subscriber growth.

Growth does not happen by accident. Setting clear goals for weekly or monthly follower growth encourages consistent posting, engagement, and outreach.

13. Posting only promotional content.

If every post promotes your services, audiences may lose interest. Social media works best when you provide value through tips, insights, and helpful resources, while occasionally promoting your services.

14. Ignoring comments and messages from followers.

Engagement builds relationships. Responding to comments and messages shows that you care about your audience and encourages people to interact with your content more often.

15. Not repurposing content across platforms.

One piece of content can often be adapted for multiple platforms. A blog post might become a short video, infographic, or series of social media posts.

16. Not building an email list from social media followers.

Social media platforms change constantly, and accounts can disappear overnight. Encouraging followers to join your email list helps you maintain direct communication with your audience.

17. Being afraid to show personality online.

People connect with people—not just information. Showing your personality helps humanize your brand and makes it easier for audiences to relate to you.

18. Using AI tools without adding personal insight.

AI tools can help generate ideas and content, but your personal experience and perspective are what make your content unique. Adding your voice and insights keeps your content authentic.

19. Not using short-form video content.

Short-form videos have become one of the fastest ways to reach new audiences. Brief, helpful videos can quickly showcase your knowledge and attract viewers who may later become clients.

20. Not linking social media activity to a clear offer.

Social media activity should ultimately lead people somewhere— your website, email list, webinar, or coaching program. Without a clear next step, you may gain followers but fail to convert them into clients.

PART 10

Website Related Mistakes

BROKE COACHES MAKE

Your website is often the first place potential clients go to learn about you and your coaching services. If your website is confusing, outdated, or poorly structured, visitors may leave before ever understanding how you can help them. The following mistakes reveal common problems that prevent coaching websites from attracting leads, building trust, and converting visitors into clients.

1. Not knowing how to properly manage your domain names.

Your domain name is the digital foundation of your business. If you lose control of it because a webmaster disappears or credentials are misplaced, recovering it can be difficult or even impossible. Every coach should know where their domains are registered and how to manage them.

2. Not building a resource center for paid clients.

A members-only resource center allows you to provide worksheets, recordings, checklists, and support materials that help clients between sessions. It adds tremendous value while allowing your coaching to continue working for clients even when you're not present.

3. Overpaying for website hosting.

Many coaches unknowingly pay far more than necessary for basic hosting. Understanding hosting plans and features can save significant money over time and prevent you from paying premium prices for services you don't actually need.

4. Not creating a private resource area for clients.

Clients often benefit from structured materials such as exercises, forms, and coaching frameworks. Providing a private area where they can easily access these tools improves the overall coaching experience and strengthens client results.

5. Having a cluttered or non-responsive website.

If visitors cannot easily navigate your website or if it doesn't display properly on phones and tablets, many will simply leave. A clean, responsive design makes it easier for potential clients to understand your services and take action.

6. Not testing your website functionality regularly.

Opt-in forms, checkout systems, booking calendars, and login pages can break without warning. Coaches who periodically test these functions ensure that potential clients never encounter frustrating technical problems.

7. Not building multiple websites to expand your brand.

Some coaches limit themselves to a single website when they could easily expand their reach through niche-specific sites, resource portals, or educational platforms that target different audiences. By creating these specialized digital touchpoints, you position yourself as a multi-dimensional expert and capture potential clients who are searching for very specific solutions rather than general advice.

8. Not creating a simple page listing your coaching packages.

Visitors should quickly understand what services you offer and how to get started. A clear overview page that outlines your coaching packages helps potential clients compare options and move toward a decision.

9. Not creating dedicated pages for each coaching package.

Each service deserves its own page where you can explain the benefits, outline the process, answer common questions, and guide visitors toward booking or purchasing the program.

10. Posting your real email address publicly on your website.

When you publish your email address openly on your website, spam bots quickly harvest it and flood your inbox with unwanted messages. Contact forms protect your email while still allowing visitors to reach you.

11. Automatically playing audio or video when visitors land on your site.

Unexpected audio can frustrate visitors and cause them to leave immediately. Allow users to choose when they want to play media instead of forcing it upon them.

12. Poor website navigation.

If visitors cannot quickly find what they're looking for, they won't stay long. Simple navigation with clear menu items helps users explore your services without confusion.

13. Poorly written web page copy.

Long paragraphs, small text, and vague headlines make websites difficult to read. Clear headlines, short paragraphs, and client-focused messaging help visitors quickly understand the value of your services.

14. Failing to place contact information in visible locations.

Some websites make it surprisingly difficult to find basic contact details. Coaches who want inquiries should make it easy for visitors to reach them by placing contact information in obvious places.

15. Broken links and images on your website.

Broken elements make a website look neglected and unprofessional. Regularly checking your links and images ensures your website maintains credibility.

16. Outdated website design.

If your website looks like it hasn't been updated in years, visitors may assume your business is no longer active. Modern design signals professionalism and trust while ensuring your authority remains clearly visible.

17. Website copy focused on you instead of the client.

Many coaching websites talk extensively about the coach but say very little about the client's problems or goals. Effective websites focus on the visitor's challenges and explain how the coach helps solve them.

18. Not learning how to manage your own hosting and accounts.

Even if you hire help, you should still understand the basics of how your website works. Knowing where files, hosting settings, and email accounts are located prevents unnecessary dependency on others.

19. Relying entirely on someone else to maintain your website.

While technical assistance is valuable, complete reliance on a webmaster can leave you vulnerable if that person becomes unavailable. Basic website knowledge gives you greater control over your business.

20. Not capturing leads with opt-in forms.

Visitors rarely become clients immediately. Email opt-ins allow you to stay connected with potential clients and build long-term relationships that may eventually lead to coaching engagements.

21. Not offering a clear call-to-action on every page.

Every page of your website should guide visitors toward the next step—booking a session, joining your list, downloading a resource, or contacting you to ensure consistent business growth.

22. Not optimizing your website for mobile devices.

A large percentage of visitors will access your website on a phone. If your site isn't optimized for mobile viewing, you risk losing a significant portion of potential clients and damaging your professional reputation.

23. Not using testimonials or success stories.

Potential clients want reassurance that your coaching produces results. Testimonials and success stories build trust and credibility.

24. Not tracking website analytics.

Analytics reveal how visitors find your site and what pages they interact with most. Without this information, it becomes difficult to improve your website's performance.

25. Not offering an easy way to schedule coaching sessions.

Modern clients expect simple online scheduling. Removing friction from the booking process makes it easier for people to become paying clients.

26. Not creating landing pages for specific offers.

Landing pages allow you to focus on a single offer without distractions. Coaches who use landing pages often see higher conversion rates when promoting programs or workshops.

PART 11

AI & Automation Mistakes

BROKE COACHES MAKE

Artificial intelligence and automation tools are rapidly changing how coaches create content, communicate with audiences, and run their businesses. When used wisely, these tools can save time, expand reach, and improve efficiency. However, relying on them incorrectly—or ignoring them altogether—can create new problems that limit growth and authenticity.

1. Ignoring AI entirely.

Some coaches refuse to learn AI tools because they think it will replace human coaching. In reality, AI can dramatically increase productivity, allowing coaches to create content faster, prepare better sessions, and serve more clients. Coaches who ignore AI risk falling behind those who embrace it.

2. Believing AI can replace real coaching.

AI can provide information, summaries, and suggestions, but it cannot replace empathy, accountability, intuition, or human understanding. Coaches who rely entirely on AI instead of human interaction weaken the value of their coaching services.

3. Using AI without verifying the information.

AI tools sometimes produce incorrect or outdated information. Coaches should always review and verify anything generated by AI before sharing it with clients or publishing it publicly.

4. Using AI-generated content without adding personal insight.

Clients follow coaches because of their experience, perspective, and personality. Simply copying and pasting AI-generated content without adding your own expertise makes your work feel generic and impersonal.

5. Not using AI to prepare for coaching sessions.

AI tools can help summarize client notes, brainstorm coaching questions, generate exercises, and organize action plans. Coaches who fail to use AI for preparation miss a powerful productivity advantage.

6. Not using AI to generate coaching resources.

AI can help create worksheets, checklists, reflection prompts, exercises, and summaries that support clients between sessions. Coaches who ignore this capability spend unnecessary time creating everything from scratch.

7. Failing to use AI for content creation.

AI can assist with writing blog posts, social media posts, newsletters, outlines for workshops, and video scripts. Coaches who learn to collaborate with AI can create content much faster and expand their reach.

8. Relying too heavily on AI prompts during coaching sessions.

While AI can help with preparation, coaching sessions should remain focused on the client's unique situation. Coaches who constantly rely on AI-generated scripts may sound robotic or disconnected.

9. Sharing confidential client information with AI tools.

Many AI platforms store prompts and conversations for training purposes. Coaches should avoid entering sensitive or identifiable client information into AI systems unless they understand the platform's privacy policies.

10. Using AI without understanding its limitations.

AI is a tool, not an authority. Coaches who assume AI always provides accurate advice risk giving poor guidance to their clients.

11. Not using AI to analyze client progress or patterns.

AI can help summarize session notes, identify recurring themes, and track progress over time. Coaches who use AI thoughtfully can gain insights that might otherwise go unnoticed.

12. Using AI to create everything instead of thinking creatively.

AI should support creativity, not replace it. Coaches who rely entirely on AI ideas may stop developing their own insights and original methods.

13. Not learning prompt writing skills.

The quality of AI results depends heavily on how questions and prompts are written. Coaches who learn to craft better prompts get far more valuable output from AI tools.

14. Failing to experiment with multiple AI tools.

Different AI tools specialize in different tasks such as writing, research, design, transcription, or video creation. Coaches who experiment with multiple platforms discover powerful combinations that save time.

15. **Using AI-generated content that sounds robotic.**

AI writing can sometimes sound mechanical or generic. Coaches should always edit and personalize AI-generated content to ensure it reflects their authentic voice.

16. **Not using AI to build scalable coaching assets.**

AI can help coaches create courses, ebooks, worksheets, and training programs faster than ever before. Coaches who ignore this opportunity limit their ability to scale their expertise.

17. **Using AI to avoid doing real work.**

AI is meant to accelerate productivity, not replace effort. Coaches who rely on AI shortcuts without understanding their own material risk weakening their expertise.

18. **Failing to disclose AI assistance when appropriate.**

Transparency builds trust. If AI significantly helps produce client materials, it may be appropriate to disclose that AI tools were used.

19. **Not using AI for research and learning.**

AI tools can summarize books, analyze ideas, explain concepts, and help coaches learn faster. Coaches who use AI for education can dramatically accelerate their own growth.

20. **Not realizing AI can increase your coaching leverage.**

AI can help coaches serve more clients, create more resources, automate repetitive work, and expand their influence. Coaches who learn to integrate AI into their workflow gain a major competitive advantage.

PART 12

Digital Coaching & Scalability Mistakes

BROKE COACHES MAKE

Many coaches begin their businesses with one-on-one sessions, but long-term growth often requires more scalable ways to deliver value. Digital programs, group coaching, courses, and online communities allow coaches to reach larger audiences while creating additional revenue streams. The following mistakes highlight common ways coaches limit their growth by failing to leverage scalable digital opportunities.

1. Relying only on one-on-one coaching sessions.

Many coaches limit their income and impact by offering only private sessions. While one-on-one coaching is valuable, it also limits the number of clients you can serve. Coaches who add scalable options such as group coaching, courses, and workshops can reach more people while increasing revenue.

2. Not offering group coaching programs.

Group coaching allows multiple clients to learn and grow together while benefiting from shared experiences. Coaches who fail to offer group programs miss an opportunity to help more people at once while generating higher income per hour.

3. Not creating digital courses.

Digital courses allow coaches to package their expertise into structured programs that clients can access anytime. Courses provide an additional income stream and allow coaches to serve clients without requiring their constant presence.

4. Failing to record coaching sessions or workshops.

Many valuable coaching insights are shared during sessions, webinars, or workshops but are never recorded. Recording sessions allows coaches to repurpose that knowledge into training programs, resources, or additional products.

5. Not building a membership community.

Membership communities create recurring revenue and ongoing engagement with clients. Coaches who fail to build a community miss an opportunity to create long-term relationships and predictable income.

6. Not automating client onboarding.

Many coaches manually send welcome emails, contracts, instructions, and resources to every new client. Automation tools can streamline this process, saving time and creating a more professional onboarding experience.

7. Failing to build systems that support growth.

Successful coaching businesses rely on systems such as scheduling software, payment processing, CRM systems, and automated communication. Without these systems, growth becomes difficult to manage.

8. Not repurposing coaching content into scalable formats.

Coaches often repeat the same insights with many clients. Those insights can be transformed into articles, videos, courses, or downloadable guides that help many people at once.

9. Trying to do everything manually.

Manual processes slow down business growth. Coaches who automate repetitive tasks such as scheduling, reminders, and content delivery free up time for higher-value activities.

10. Not offering recorded training libraries.

Clients often benefit from reviewing lessons multiple times. Creating a library of recorded lessons, workshops, or tutorials adds tremendous value and reduces repetitive explanations.

11. Not building a digital resource library.

Checklists, worksheets, templates, and exercises can dramatically enhance coaching results. Coaches who build resource libraries help clients stay engaged between sessions.

12. Not using online scheduling tools.

Scheduling back-and-forth emails wastes time. Online scheduling tools simplify appointment booking and eliminate unnecessary communication.

13. Not offering hybrid coaching models.

Many successful coaches combine digital programs with live coaching sessions. Hybrid models allow clients to learn foundational material on their own time while using coaching sessions for deeper support.

14. Failing to track client progress digitally.

Digital tracking tools can help clients monitor their progress, goals, and accountability tasks. Coaches who use these tools help clients stay more engaged and committed.

15. Not creating structured coaching frameworks.

When coaching is unstructured, it becomes difficult to scale. Creating repeatable frameworks allows coaches to deliver consistent results while expanding their services.

16. Ignoring opportunities to license your coaching methods.

If your coaching approach produces strong results, it may be possible to license your system to other coaches. Licensing allows your methodology to reach more clients without requiring your direct involvement.

17. Not training other coaches to deliver your system.

Some coaches build powerful systems but never teach others how to implement them. Training certified coaches can expand your brand and increase your influence.

18. Not building a digital audience.

Scalable coaching businesses often rely on audiences built through newsletters, podcasts, YouTube channels, or social media. Coaches who ignore audience building limit their long-term reach.

19. Trying to scale too quickly without structure.

Rapid growth without systems can overwhelm coaches and damage client experiences. Scaling successfully requires clear processes, systems, and support structures.

20. Not realizing your coaching knowledge can scale far beyond your time.

Your ideas, frameworks, and lessons can reach thousands of people through books, courses, workshops, and digital programs. Coaches who recognize this opportunity dramatically expand their impact and income.

Start Here: The 10 Most Expensive Coaching Mistakes!!!

Whether you are a new coach or a seasoned professional, certain mistakes can quietly derail your progress. Many struggle financially not from a lack of talent, but because of a few expensive errors. Before proceeding, review these 10 costly coaching mistakes. Avoiding even a handful can dramatically improve your chances of building a successful, thriving business.

1. Trying to help everyone instead of choosing a niche. Many coaches believe they must appeal to everyone. Actually, specializing in a specific group and problem makes your message more powerful.

2. Waiting for clients to magically appear. Coaching is not a "build it and they will come" profession. Successful coaches consistently market their services, build relationships, create content, and actively look for opportunities to help others.

3. Underpricing your coaching services. Coaches undervalue services from lack of confidence or fear. Ironically, charging too little attracts wrong clients and makes sustaining a business difficult.

4. Failing to build an audience. Your audience is your future clients. Coaches who consistently build audiences through content, speaking, writing, or email dramatically increase their opportunities.

5. Relying only on one-on-one coaching sessions. Private coaching can be valuable, but it limits how many clients you can serve. Coaches who expand into group coaching, courses, workshops, and digital programs create scalable income and reach more people.

6. **Not learning how to sell.** Many coaches feel uncomfortable discussing money or asking for the sale. However, selling is simply the process of helping someone decide to invest in solving their problem.

7. **Ignoring technology and modern tools.** Technology and AI dramatically improve efficiency and reach. Coaches who refuse to adapt risk falling behind those who embrace new tools.

8. **Trying to do everything alone.** Successful coaches build networks, partnerships, and collaborations. Working with other professionals can open doors to new clients, new audiences, and new opportunities.

9. **Failing to learn from mistakes.** Mistakes are inevitable. The most successful coaches don't avoid them entirely—they learn quickly and adjust their approach.

10. **Forgetting that coaching is about helping people.** The most successful coaching practices are built on helping others. When coaches focus on serving people well, business success often follows naturally.

A Final Thought Before You Begin

Every coach makes mistakes, which are often the fastest way to gain wisdom. The goal of this book is to help you recognize common pitfalls so you can avoid them and grow faster. You may discover mistakes you've already made or are currently making, but these lessons will help you become a stronger, more successful coach. Now let's get started.

SUMMARY & WORDS
OF ENCOURAGEMENT

I hope you've learned a lot from reviewing these *150+ MISTAKES THAT COACHES MAKE!!!*

Some of them may have made you nod your head and say, "Yes, I've done that." Others may have surprised you. Perhaps a few may have opened your eyes to mistakes you didn't even realize coaches commonly make. That's the purpose of this book.

Mistakes are not something to fear. In fact, they are one of the greatest teachers any professional can have. Every successful coach, business owner, consultant, or entrepreneur has made countless mistakes along the way. The difference between those who succeed and those who struggle is simple: successful people **learn from their mistakes and improve quickly**.

Now that you've been introduced to these common coaching mistakes, you are far better prepared to recognize them early—or avoid them altogether. By understanding these pitfalls, you gain the foresight to navigate your professional journey with greater confidence and strategic clarity. This awareness allows you to protect your practice from unnecessary setbacks and ensures that your energy is focused entirely on delivering the high-value results your clients deserve. You'll notice that many of the mistakes in this book fall into a few important categories:

- **Business mistakes** that prevent coaches from building sustainable practices ...

- **Marketing mistakes** that make it harder for people to discover their services ...

- **Mindset mistakes** that hold coaches back from reaching their full potential ...

- **Technology mistakes** that limit growth in today's digital world ...

- **Personal mistakes** that affect energy, confidence, and long-term success ...

The truth is that becoming a great coach is not about being perfect. It's about **constantly improving**. The best coaches in the world are students of their craft. They continue learning, adapting, experimenting, and refining their methods. They pay attention to what works, and they quickly adjust when something doesn't.

As you grow your coaching practice, you will likely encounter new challenges, new opportunities, and yes—new mistakes. That's perfectly normal. What matters most is how quickly you recognize those situations and use them as opportunities to grow. If you take one idea away from this book, let it be this:

FOCUS ON HELPING PEOPLE FIRST

When you genuinely care about helping your clients achieve meaningful progress in their lives, many other things fall into place—your reputation grows, referrals increase, and your coaching practice becomes stronger over time.

The world needs great coaches. People everywhere are looking for guidance, clarity, encouragement, and accountability. They want someone who will listen, challenge them, and help them move forward. If you stay committed to learning, improving, and serving others well, your coaching career can be incredibly rewarding—both personally and professionally.

I encourage you to keep growing, keep experimenting, and keep helping people achieve their goals. And when you discover new lessons along your journey, remember that those experiences—both successes and mistakes—are part of what makes you a better coach.

I'd really like to hear about your progress and your success stories along the way. You can reach me online at my website.

To your continued success,

Bart Smith

BARTSMITH.COM
CoachingClientForms.com
RichCoachBrokeCoach.com
MyChecklistBook.com
LethalConfidence.com
... and others!

MY "RICH COACH BOOK"

If you really want to take your coaching business to the next level, then you need my **RICH COACH ◆ BROKE COACH** book. For aspiring and current coaches, *Rich Coach Broke Coach* was written with the intent on helping coaches where they need it most: in the areas of business, marketing, client interactions, sales, and making money.

Rich Coach Broke Coach is your blueprint for all that and much more. What you'll find inside this rich manual is only the most concise, nugget-rich content you have probably ever read on running a profitable coaching business. This book is strictly about improving the "business aspect" of your coaching profession.

TOPICS INCLUDE:

Income & Setting Your Fees

Creating Coaching Packages

Contracts & Agreements

Finding Clients

Enrolling Clients

Overcoming Objections

Working With Clients

Coaching Resources

Marketing Tactics

... and much more!

You can learn more about this one-of-a-kind coaching business manual and order it (in print and/or audio format) at my website:

RichCoachBrokeCoach.com

MY "RICH COACH FORMS"

Every coach (i.e., life, personal and/or business coach) needs their own set of customized coaching/client agreement/assessment forms to help run a successful coaching business. Because many coaches, and those who aspire to be coaches, don't have such forms or know how to create them, I have taken the time to create (and share) the same ones I use with you.

Peruse the following list of coaching forms. It's very complete and the perfect set of forms to launch any coaching business successfully. Each of the forms you see below are for sale separately or as a COMPLETE COACHING & AGREEMENT FORMS BUNDLE, which SAVES YOU OVER $125. Cost? *Just $30 at my website!*

1. *Welcome Letter*
2. *Coaching Client Agreement*
3. *Client Intake Form*
4. *Client Self-Assessment Form*
5. *Free Coaching Gift Certificates*
6. *Free Coaching Session Agreement*
7. *Coaching Session Preparation Form*
8. *Coaching Session Summary Forms*
9. *Client Call Record (For The Coach)*
10. *The Wheel Of Life Form*
11. *Goals & Action Questions*
12. *Coaching Period Summary Forms*
13. *Client Feedback/Testimonial Form*
14. *Coaching / Speaking Hour Log (Excel)*

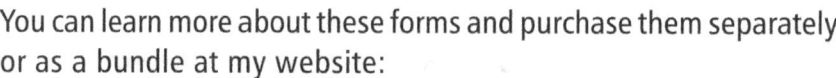

You can learn more about these forms and purchase them separately or as a bundle at my website:

CoachingClientForms.com

ABOUT THE AUTHOR
Bart Smith

BART SMITH is an entrepreneur, author, and longtime web strategist who has spent more than two decades studying how businesses operate online—and why many of them struggle to turn their expertise into consistent income.

Over the years he has built websites, written dozens of business books, and worked closely with authors, coaches and speakers across many industries. Through that experience he began noticing a recurring pattern: many talented professionals — especially coaches — were excellent at helping others but often struggled with the business side of their own practices.

That realization led Bart to write **Rich Coach • Broke Coach**, a "rich with coaching knowledge" manual designed to help life, personal, and business coaches build profitable coaching businesses. The book focuses on the areas where many coaches feel least prepared—marketing, pricing, client management, and creating consistent revenue. Rather than offering abstract theory, the book delivers straightforward business and marketing strategies for structuring coaching services, attracting clients, and building sustainable income streams.

While developing the book, Bart also saw that many coaches lacked organized systems for managing their coaching client relationships. To address this, he created a set of 14 structured coaching client forms, including intake forms, coaching agreements, session logs, and client progress tools. These forms were designed to help coaches run their practices more professionally, stay organized, and create clear structure in their client work.

Beyond the coaching industry, Bart has written **35+ books** focused on entrepreneurship, marketing, business strategy, confidence, controlling ones emotions, motivation, relationships, and identifying costly business mistakes that hold professional coaches back. His books, eBooks and audiobooks often emphasize practical action and structured thinking — helping readers avoid common pitfalls and build stronger, more sustainable businesses.

Bart's perspective is shaped by more than 20 years of experience as an online strategist, where he has observed firsthand how businesses succeed — or fail — online. That long-term vantage point has allowed him to recognize the patterns and mistakes entrepreneurs repeatedly make when building service-based businesses. Through his books, tools, and training materials, Smith focuses on a simple mission → helping professionals avoid costly mistakes, think more strategically, and build businesses that truly work.

When he isn't writing or building new projects, Bart enjoys studying marketing trends, experimenting with new business ideas, cooking (BartsCookbook.com), and baking his world famous chocolate chip cookies (BartsCookies.com) — proof that even serious strategists appreciate life's sweeter moments. You Can learn more about Bart's work and projects at:

BARTSMITH.COM

www.ingramcontent.com/pod-product-compliance
Lightning Source LLC
Chambersburg PA
CBHW071821200526
45169CB00018B/575